D1159139

ALL AROUND THE WORLD
ENGLAND

by Jessica Dean

Ideas for Parents and Teachers

Pogo Books let children practice reading informational text while introducing them to nonfiction features such as headings, labels, sidebars, maps, and diagrams, as well as a table of contents, glossary, and index.

Carefully leveled text with a strong photo match offers early fluent readers the support they need to succeed.

Before Reading

- "Walk" through the book and point out the various nonfiction features. Ask the student what purpose each feature serves.
- Look at the glossary together. Read and discuss the words.

Read the Book

- Have the child read the book independently.
- Invite him or her to list questions that arise from reading.

After Reading

- Discuss the child's questions. Talk about how he or she might find answers to those questions.
- Prompt the child to think more. Ask: People all over the world like to read about England's royal family. Why do you think that is?

Pogo Books are published by Jump!
5357 Penn Avenue South
Minneapolis, MN 55419
www.jumplibrary.com

Library of Congress Cataloging-in-Publication Data

Names: Dean, Jessica, 1963- author.
Title: England / by Jessica Dean.
Description: Pogo books. | Minneapolis, MN : Jump!, [2019]
Series: All around the world | Includes index.
Audience: Ages 7-10.
Identifiers: LCCN 2018014524 (print)
LCCN 2018014959 (ebook)
ISBN 9781641281546 (ebook)
ISBN 9781641281522 (hardcover : alk. paper)
ISBN 9781641281539 (pbk.)
Subjects: LCSH: England—Juvenile literature.
Classification: LCC DA27.5 (ebook)
LCC DA27.5 .D425 2019 (print) | DDC 942—dc23
LC record available at https://lccn.loc.gov/2018014524

Editor: Kristine Spanier
Designer: Molly Ballanger

Photo Credits: Ratiokva/Shutterstock, cover; Sandra Mori/Shutterstock, 1; Pixfiction/Shutterstock, 3; kentaylordesign/Shutterstock, 4; Shaiith/iStock, 5; Patryk Kosmider/Shutterstock, 6-7; Coatesy/Shutterstock, 8tl; Alan De Witt/Shutterstock, 8-9t; David Cole/age fotostock/SuperStock, 8bl; Rudmer Zwerver/Shutterstock, 8-9b; Edward Haylan/Shutterstock, 10; Giancarlo Liguori/Shutterstock, 11; Chris Jackson/Getty, 12-13, 17; Caiaimage/Chris Ryan/Getty, 14-15; Brian A Jackson/Shutterstock, 16; JoeGough/iStock, 18-19; Marco Iacobucci EPP/Shutterstock, 20-21; incamerastock/Alamy, 23.

Printed in the United States of America at Corporate Graphics in North Mankato, Minnesota.

TABLE OF CONTENTS

CHAPTER 1
Welcome to England! 4

CHAPTER 2
Life in England 10

CHAPTER 3
Holidays, Food, and Fun 16

QUICK FACTS & TOOLS
At a Glance 22
Glossary 23
Index 24
To Learn More 24

CHAPTER 1

WELCOME TO ENGLAND!

Choose a castle to visit.
Explore historic **landmarks**.
Eat fish and chips for lunch.
Welcome to England!

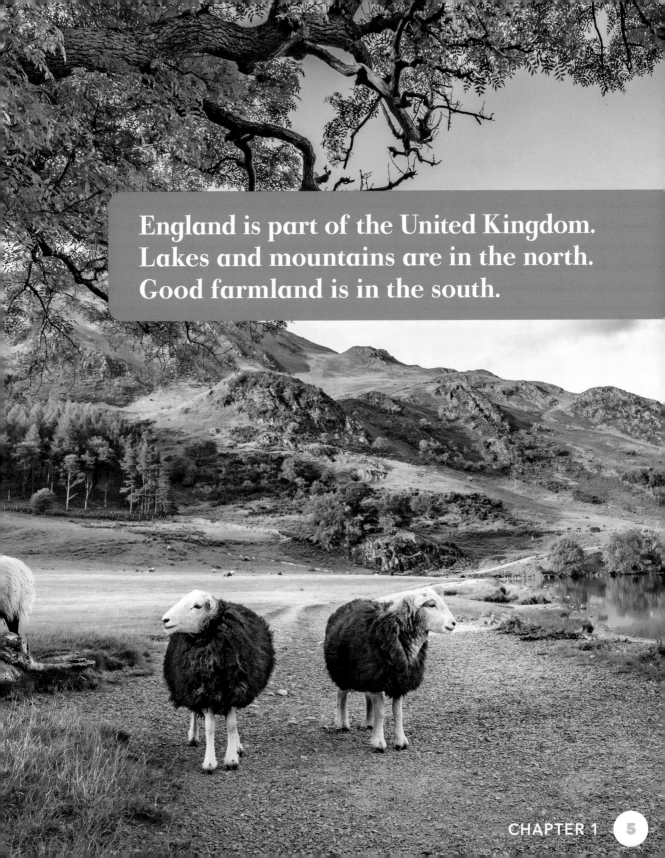

England is part of the United Kingdom. Lakes and mountains are in the north. Good farmland is in the south.

England has rocky coastlines and **marshes**. The Jurassic Coast borders the English Channel. People still look for **fossils** here.

Winters are cold and wet. Summers are warm. Weather moves in quickly from the sea.

DID YOU KNOW?

An underwater tunnel was built in the English Channel. It is called the Chunnel. It transports people via train between England and France in only 30 minutes!

hedgehog

gray seal

pipistrelle bat

pygmy shrew

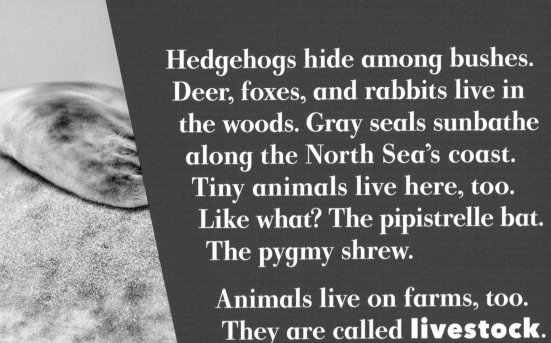

Hedgehogs hide among bushes. Deer, foxes, and rabbits live in the woods. Gray seals sunbathe along the North Sea's coast. Tiny animals live here, too. Like what? The pipistrelle bat. The pygmy shrew.

Animals live on farms, too. They are called **livestock**. Beef cattle are here. So are dairy cows. Sheep. Pigs.

CHAPTER 2
LIFE IN ENGLAND

People live in small towns and big cities. One town is Amesbury. Stonehenge is here. It is a **prehistoric** monument.

Stonehenge

London is the **capital**. It is one of the biggest cities in the world. The River Thames runs through it. The **prime minister** heads the government. Lawmakers meet in the Palace of Westminster. It has a bell and clock tower. People call it Big Ben.

Big Ben

Palace of Westminster

royal family

England was once ruled by a **monarchy**. The royal family is now active in **charity** work. Buckingham Palace is home to the **sovereign**.

DID YOU KNOW?

A flypast is a flight of Royal Air Force planes. Flypasts honor special events and people. The royal family watches flypasts from the Buckingham Palace balcony.

Children start school by age five. Most students wear uniforms. At age 16 they may leave school. Others stay for two more years to prepare for college. Some train to work in **trades**.

Most English workers have **service jobs** like banking or teaching. Other people work in factories.

WHAT DO YOU THINK?

What are the benefits of uniforms? Would you like dressing the same as other students? Do you think there are drawbacks?

CHAPTER 3

HOLIDAYS, FOOD, AND FUN

Some occasions in England mark moments in history. People wear poppies on November 11 for Remembrance Day. This honors people who lost their lives in World War I (1914–1918) and World War II (1939–1945).

poppy ·····▶

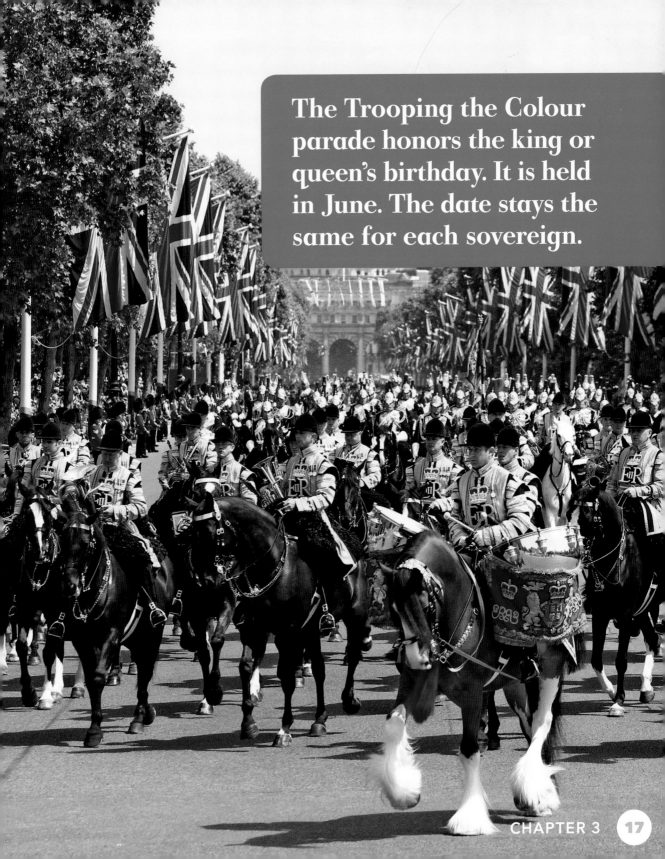

The Trooping the Colour parade honors the king or queen's birthday. It is held in June. The date stays the same for each sovereign.

Yorkshire pudding

English food is filling. A favorite lunch sandwich is the bacon butty. Bacon and ketchup are layered inside bread. Dinner might be roast beef with Yorkshire pudding.

Tea is both a drink and a meal. Cookies or sandwiches are served with it. Even children drink tea!

TAKE A LOOK!

In England, common foods are known by names that may be different from those you use.

IF YOU WANT...　　　　　**ASK FOR...**

 French fries → chips

 potato chips → crisps

 cookies → biscuits

 grilled cheese → toastie

 cupcakes → fairy cakes

rugby

Rugby is a popular sport here. Soccer is called football. English football teams are called clubs. Club fans are loud and loyal. People also play tennis and cricket.

There is so much to experience here. What would you like to do in England?

WHAT DO YOU THINK?

Long ago, people watched knights on horseback fight one another. Would you rather watch knights or rugby players? Why?

QUICK FACTS & TOOLS

AT A GLANCE

ENGLAND

Location: Western Europe

Size: 50,539 square miles (130,895 square kilometers)

Population: 55,268,067 (July 2017 estimate)

Capital: London

Type of Government: parliamentary constitutional monarchy

Language: English

Exports: fuels, food, chemicals

Currency: pound sterling

GLOSSARY

capital: A city where government leaders meet.

charity: Aid given to those in need.

fossils: Traces, prints, or the remains of ancient plants or animals that are saved in soil or rock.

landmarks: Objects in landscapes that stand out.

livestock: Animals that are kept or raised on a farm or ranch.

marshes: Areas of wet, muddy land.

monarchy: A government in which the head of state is a king or queen.

prehistoric: Belonging to a time before history was recorded in written form.

prime minister: The leader of a country.

rugby: A form of football played by two teams that kick, pass, or carry an oval ball.

service jobs: Jobs and work that provide services for others, such as hotel, restaurant, and retail positions.

sovereign: A king or queen.

trades: Particular jobs, especially those that require working with the hands or machines.

England's currency

INDEX

Amesbury 10

animals 9

Big Ben 11

Buckingham Palace 13

Chunnel 6

English Channel 6

flypast 13

food 4, 18, 19

France 6

Jurassic Coast 6

landmarks 4

livestock 9

London 11

monarchy 13

Palace of Westminster 11

prime minister 11

Remembrance Day 16

River Thames 11

school 14

service jobs 14

sovereign 13, 17

sport 21

Stonehenge 10

trades 14

Trooping the Colour 17

United Kingdom 5

TO LEARN MORE

Learning more is as easy as 1, 2, 3.

1) Go to www.factsurfer.com

2) Enter "England" into the search box.

3) Click the "Surf" button to see a list of websites.

With factsurfer, finding more information is just a click away.